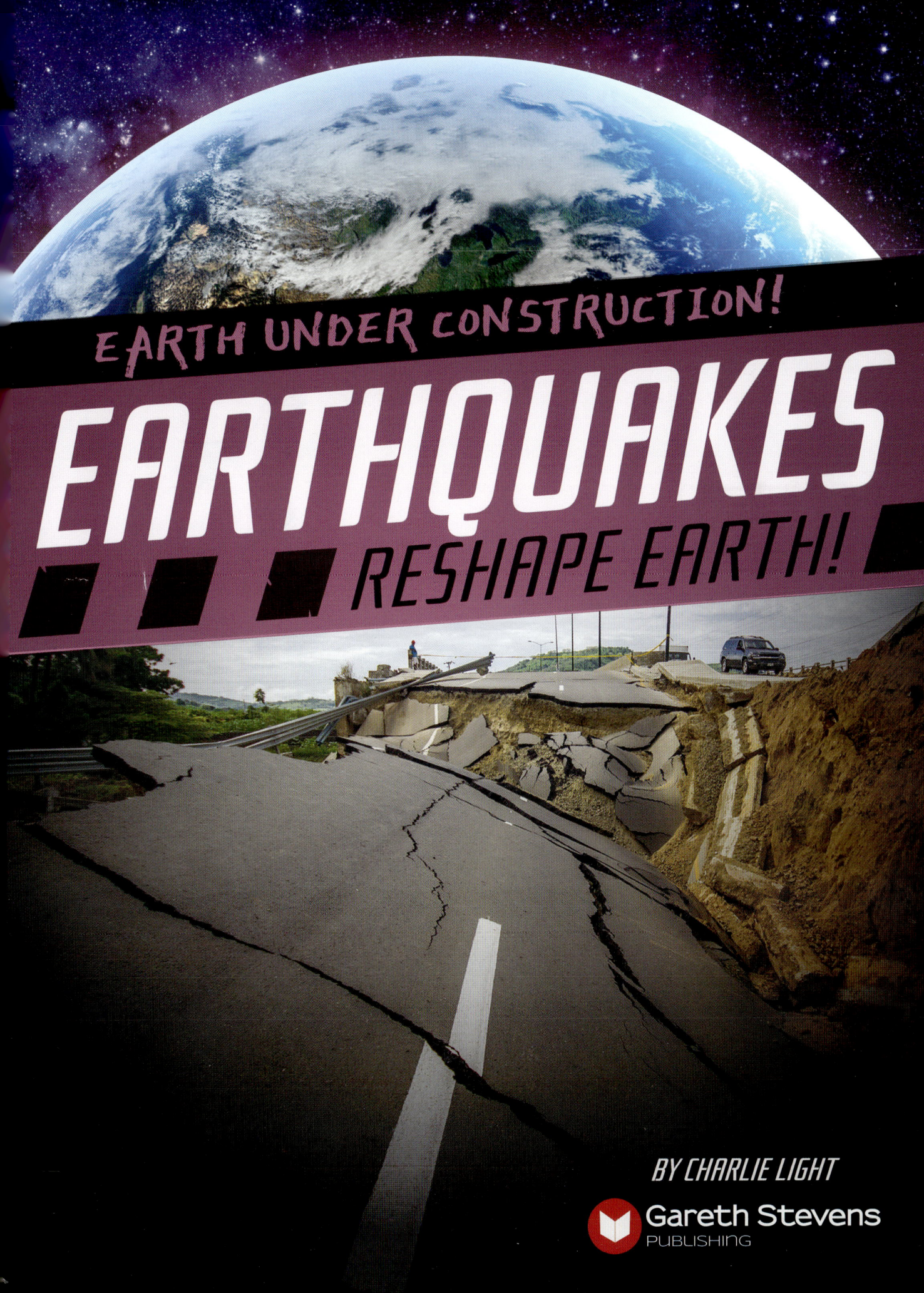

EARTH UNDER CONSTRUCTION!

EARTHQUAKES
RESHAPE EARTH!

BY CHARLIE LIGHT

Gareth Stevens
PUBLISHING

Please visit our website, www.garethstevens.com. For a free color catalog of all our high-quality books, call toll free 1-800-542-2595 or fax 1-877-542-2596.

Library of Congress Cataloging-in-Publication Data

Names: Light, Charlie, author.
Title: Earthquakes reshape Earth! / Charlie Light.
Description: New York : Gareth Stevens Publishing, 2021. | Series: Earth under construction! | Includes bibliographical references and index. | Contents: What is an earthquake? – Earth's layers – Energy causes earthquakes – Body waves – Surface waves – Measuring earthquakes – Tectonic earthquakes – Plate boundaries – Volcanic earthquakes– Humans can cause earthquakes – Effects of earthquakes – Earthquakes cause disasters – Earthquake engineering.
Identifiers: LCCN 2020000611 | ISBN 9781538258408 (library binding) | ISBN 9781538258385 (paperback) | ISBN 9781538258392 (6 Pack) | ISBN 9781538258415 (ebook)
Subjects: LCSH: Earthquakes–Juvenile literature. | Earthquakes–Social aspects–Juvenile literature. | Earthquakes–Environmental aspects–Juvenile literature.
Classification: LCC QE521.3 .L54 2020 | DDC 551.22–dc23
LC record available at https://lccn.loc.gov/2020000611

First Edition

Published in 2021 by
Gareth Stevens Publishing
111 East 14th Street, Suite 349
New York, NY 10003

Designer: Sarah Liddell
Editor: Kate Mikoley

Photo credits: Cover, p. 1 Fotos593/Shutterstock.com; space background and Earth image used throughout Aphelleon/Shutterstock.com; caution tape used throughout Red sun design/Shutterstock.com; p. 5 Anadolu Agency/Contributor/Anadolu/Getty Images; p. 7 Rost9/Shutterstock.com; p. 9 Gary S Chapman/DigitalVision/Getty Images; p. 11 Tudor Costache/Moment/Getty Images; p. 13 SalvagorGali/Shutterstock.com; p. 15 Bettmann/Contributor/Bettmann/Getty Images; p. 17 Morley Read/Photolibrary/Getty Images Plus/Getty images; p. 19 Kevin Schafer/The Image Bank/Getty Images; p. 21 SCIENCE PHOTO LIBRARY/Science Photo Library/Getty Images Plus/Getty Images; p. 23 Jesse Kraft/EyeEm/EyeEm/Getty Images; p. 25 (top) Haje Jan Kamps/EyeEm/EyeEm/Getty Images; p. 25 (bottom) DEA/BIBLIOTECA AMBROSIANA/Contributor/De Agostini/Getty Images; p. 27 KAZUHIRO NOGI/Staff/AFP/Getty Images; p. 29 NOEL CELIS/Stringer/AFP/Getty Images.

Printed in the United States of America

Some of the images in this book illustrate individuals who are models. The depictions do not imply actual situations or events.

CPSIA compliance information: Batch #CS20GS: For further information contact Gareth Stevens, New York, New York at 1-800-542-2595.

Find us on

CONTENTS

Words in the glossary appear in **bold** type the first time they are used in the text.

WHAT IS AN EARTHQUAKE?

An earthquake is exactly what it sounds like—it's the earth quaking, or shaking! Earthquakes are caused by bursts of energy in Earth's crust. This is the layer of Earth where we live. It's made up of dry land and oceans. The part of Earth's surface made up of dry land is called continental crust. Land below oceans is called oceanic crust. Earthquakes can happen in both.

Earth has many layers. The crust is at the top. It's broken into big parts called tectonic plates. These are like a hard shell on the outside of the planet. Tectonic plates are moving slowly all the time.

THE DEADLIEST EARTHQUAKE OF 2019 HAPPENED IN ALBANIA. FIFTY-ONE PEOPLE DIED. ABOUT 2,000 PEOPLE WERE HURT AND 4,000 PEOPLE LOST THEIR HOMES.

SHAKING THE SURFACE

Earthquakes happen all the time—**literally**! There's always an earthquake happening somewhere. Hundreds of small earthquakes happen every day. These earthquakes usually don't cause **damage**. Earthquakes that cause damage, called major earthquakes, happen every month. The biggest earthquakes are called great earthquakes. About one great earthquake happens each year.

5

EARTH'S LAYERS

The crust floats on top of the mantle. The mantle makes up more than 80 percent of Earth's volume! The part where the crust and mantle meet is called the lithosphere. The top of the mantle is partly **molten**. It's called the asthenosphere. The lower mantle is mostly solid.

Below the mantle is Earth's core. It has an outer part that is liquid. The inner core is solid. Scientists think it's solid because it's under so much pressure.

Earth's core is very hot. It can reach 10,800°F (6,000°C). That's as hot as the sun's surface!

LAYERS OF THE EARTH

CRUST —————

ASTHENOSPHERE

MANTLE —————

INNER CORE —————

OUTER CORE —————

LITHOSPHERE

TECTONIC PLATES MOVE BECAUSE OF BUILT UP ENERGY UNDER EARTH'S SURFACE. THIS ENERGY IS CALLED TENSION.

EARTH'S MOVING CONTINENTS

Earth's crust has seven big masses of land. They're called continents. The continents are Antarctica, Africa, Asia, Australia, Europe, North America, and South America. The continents ride on tectonic plates. Scientists think there used to be one big continent called Pangea (also spelled Pangaea). As the plates moved, Pangea broke into smaller continents.

7

ENERGY CAUSES EARTHQUAKES

Earthquakes are waves of energy moving through Earth. They start with a burst of energy in Earth's crust. The energy flows through the rocks. It moves in waves of **vibration**. These are called seismic waves.

There are two main kinds of seismic waves. These are body waves and surface waves. Body waves move through Earth's inner layers. You can think of it as waves inside Earth's body! Body waves hit first. Surface waves come next. Surface waves move along Earth's crust. They cause the most damage. There are different kinds of body and surface waves.

SEISMOGRAPH

THE STUDY OF EARTHQUAKES IS CALLED SEISMOLOGY. SCIENTISTS WHO STUDY SEISMOLOGY ARE CALLED SEISMOLOGISTS.

SEISMOGRAPH

Scientists use a tool called a seismograph to measure seismic waves. These waves are what make up an earthquake. A seismograph measures the amplitude of waves. This is how powerful the wave is. It also measures the frequency of the waves. This is how often the waves are happening.

9

BODY WAVES

There are two kinds of body waves—primary waves and secondary waves. Primary means first. Secondary means coming in second. This is the order these waves hit an area. They're called P waves and S waves for short.

P waves are the fastest seismic waves. That's why they always hit first. They can move through solids, liquids, and gases. They push and pull rock as they move through it. P waves move through the air as sound waves. Humans can sometimes feel these waves as bumps.

S waves can only move through solids. They move rocks up and down or side to side.

CAN ANIMALS SENSE EARTHQUAKES?

Have you ever heard of animals sensing earthquakes before they happen? Some animals can hear body waves in the earth. People can't hear them. This means some animals can tell an earthquake is happening before humans notice. Animals may start acting strangely before the surface waves get there.

11

SURFACE WAVES

Surface waves hit after body waves. They move along the top of Earth, rather than in its inner layers like body waves. Deeper earthquakes often don't have surface waves.

The two kinds of surface waves are Love waves and Rayleigh waves. Love waves are the fastest surface waves. They move the ground from side to side.

Rayleigh waves move like waves in the sea. They roll through the ground the way waves roll across water. Rayleigh waves move the ground up and down. They can also move it from side to side. People feel Rayleigh waves the most. They cause most of the shaking. This is because they're the largest of all the waves.

WAVES IN MOTION

P WAVE

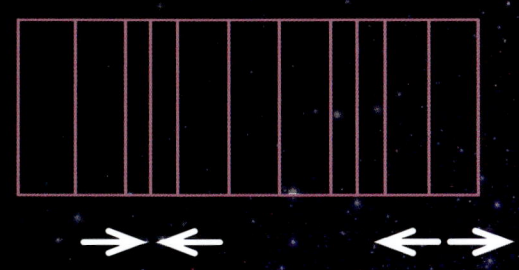

S WAVE

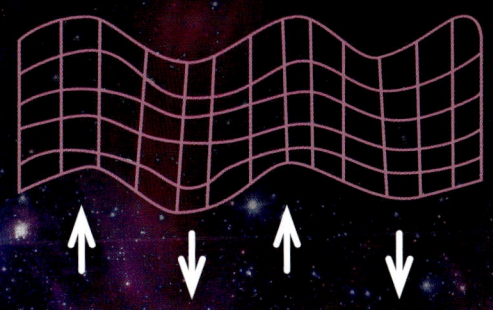

RAYLEIGH WAVE

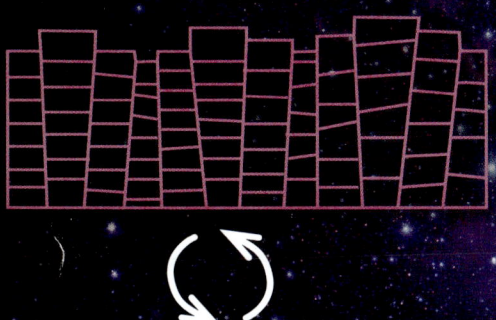

LOVE WAVE

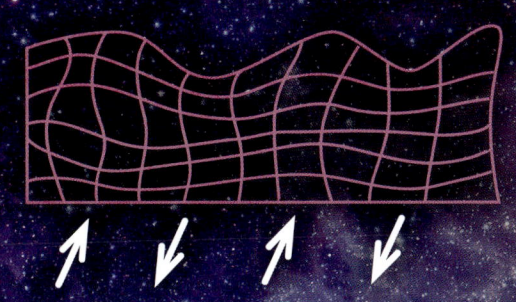

THE ARROWS ABOVE SHOW THE DIRECTION THE WAVES MOVE THE EARTH. P WAVES MAKE THE GROUND CONTRACT, OR PUSH TOGETHER, AND STRETCH APART. S WAVES MOVE ROCKS UP AND DOWN AS THEY PASS THROUGH. RAYLEIGH WAVES ROLL THROUGH ROCKS, WHILE LOVE WAVES MOVE ROCKS SIDE TO SIDE AS THEY PASS THROUGH.

DO SEISMOLOGISTS "LOVE" EARTHQUAKES?

Love can seem like a funny name for seismic waves. They do a lot of damage, after all! These waves are named after British scientist Augustus Edward Hough Love. He was the first person to find this kind of seismic wave. Rayleigh waves were named after Lord Rayleigh. He found these waves first.

13

MEASURING EARTHQUAKES

Seismologists use a scale when they measure earthquakes. This helps them measure how powerful each earthquake is. This includes how much damage each earthquake does. An earthquake's power is called its magnitude. The first earthquake magnitude scale was made by Charles Richter in the 1930s. It was called the Richter scale.

Seismologists found that the Richter scale could only measure some earthquakes. It missed a lot of information. They began measuring the magnitude of body waves and surface waves too. Then they put all these different measurements into one scale. This is called the moment magnitude scale.

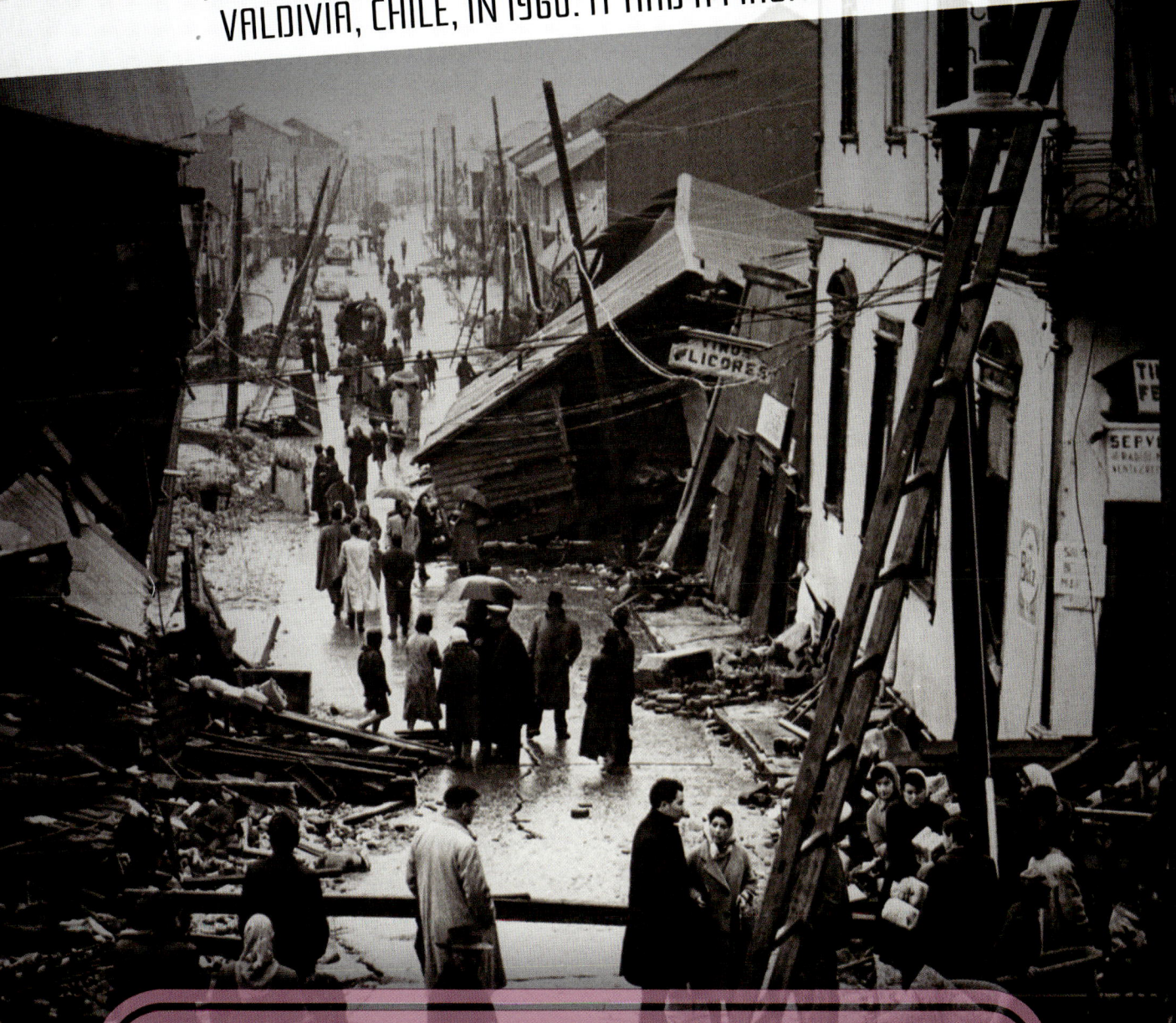

THE BIGGEST EARTHQUAKE EVER RECORDED HAPPENED IN VALDIVIA, CHILE, IN 1960. IT HAD A MAGNITUDE OF 9.5.

EARTHQUAKES BY THE NUMBERS

The magnitude scale gives earthquakes a number. The smallest quakes are 2.5 or less. Earthquakes above a 6 can cause a lot of damage. The biggest earthquakes are 8 or greater. The moment magnitude scale is the only scale that can measure quakes above an 8.

15

TECTONIC EARTHQUAKES

Tectonic plates are always moving very slowly. The plates can rub against each other as they move. They can even get stuck. Sometimes plates push against each other. This pushing energy builds and builds. Suddenly, the rock breaks from the pressure. The plates move past each other very quickly. This gives off a burst of energy. It moves through the earth as seismic waves. These waves are an earthquake!

Earthquakes that start this way are called tectonic earthquakes. They're the most common kind of earthquake. Tectonic earthquakes happen where tectonic plates meet. These places are called plate boundaries.

MOVEMENT MAKES THINGS

Tectonic plates can cause earthquakes when they push together. This movement can make other things too! When tectonic plates push together, they can build mountains. This happens when one plate rides on top of another plate. When plates pull apart, they can make new landmasses. Sometimes, a tectonic earthquake can even make a volcano erupt by putting more pressure on an area that holds magma.

17

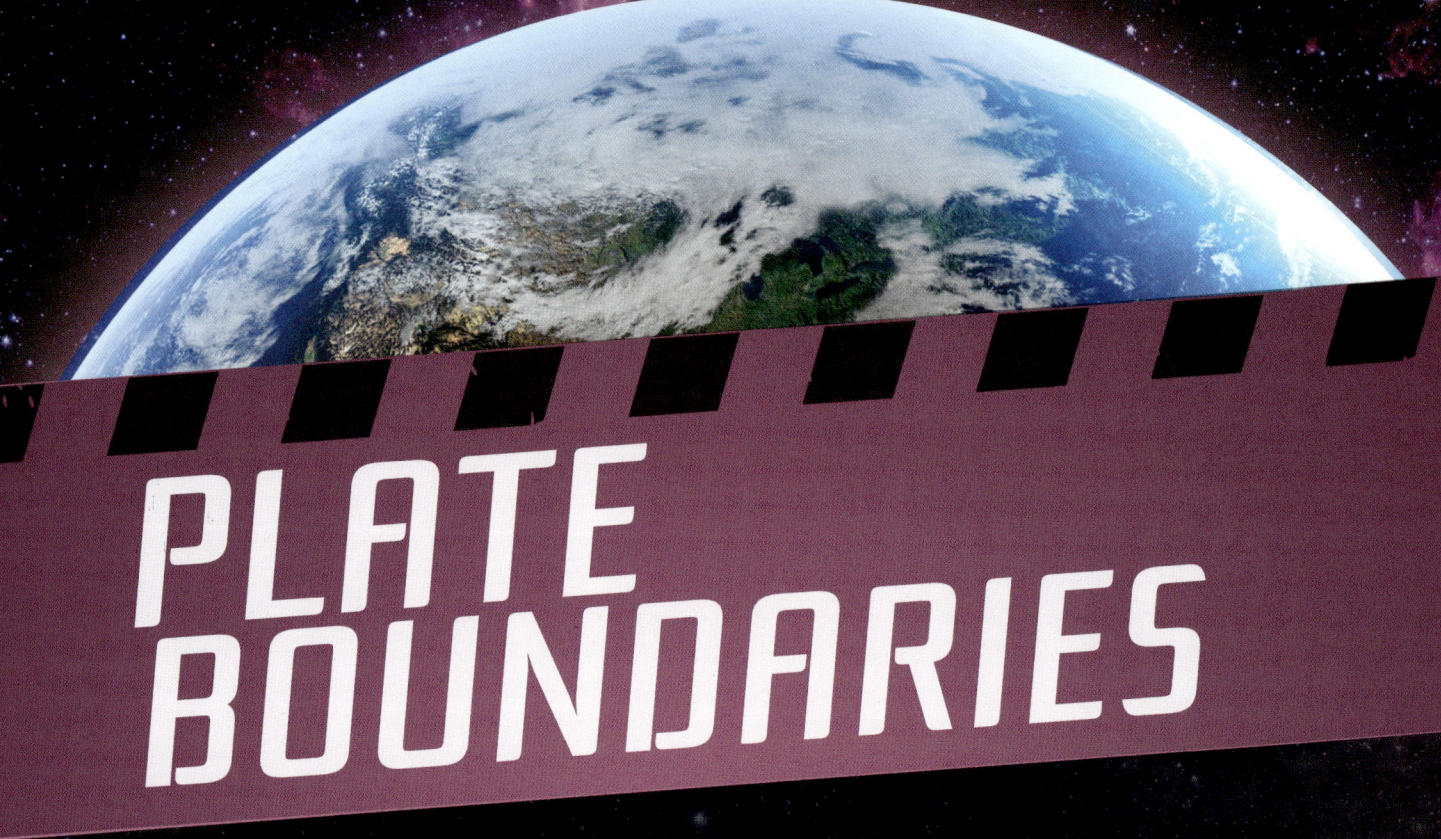

PLATE BOUNDARIES

Plates can move past each other in different ways, often causing earthquakes. These movements cause different types of plate boundaries to form.

Convergent boundaries happen when plates push together. One plate "slips," or goes under the other. The other plate rides on top of the slipped plate. The Andes Mountains are caused by a convergent boundary.

Divergent boundaries happen when two plates pull away from each other. Magma, rising from the mantle to the surface, cools and forms new crust. A divergent boundary caused the **Mid-Atlantic Ridge**.

Transform boundaries occur when plates move past each other. This makes zigzag edges on the plates. The San Andreas Fault in California is an example of a transform boundary.

WHOSE "FAULT" IS IT?

Faults are cracks between two chunks of rock. Faults between tectonic plates let them move past each other. Faults can form fault lines. These are lines in Earth's crust where the crust has moved. An area with lots of fault lines is called a fault zone.

19

VOLCANIC EARTHQUAKES

Volcanoes can also cause earthquakes. These are called volcanic earthquakes. They often happen when there is a fault near a volcano. These are usually caused by the movement of dense magma and its heat as it rises.

This happens directly below a volcano. The dense magma pushes on rocks until they break. It fills the cracks in the rocks. It builds more pressure until the rocks break again. Each time the rock breaks, an earthquake happens. The release of gas under pressure caused by magma pools can also cause earthquakes. These earthquakes are usually too small for people to feel. They're called volcano-tectonic (VT) earthquakes.

EARTHQUAKES AND VOLCANOES ARE OFTEN CONNECTED. IN 1980, AN EARTHQUAKE LED TO MOUNT ST. HELENS ERUPTING. IT WAS THE DEADLIEST ERUPTION IN U.S. HISTORY.

EARTHQUAKES BEFORE ERUPTIONS

Scientists who study volcanoes are called volcanologists. They watch out for earthquakes to tell when a volcano will erupt, which can release poisonous gases and cause destructive lava flows. One kind of earthquake is called a harmonic tremor. This is a small shaking that doesn't stop. It's a sign the volcano will erupt soon!

21

HUMANS CAN CAUSE EARTHQUAKES

Human activity can also cause earthquakes. The most common activity that causes earthquakes is filling **reservoirs** with water. Reservoirs hold huge amounts of water. Tall walls called dams hold the water in place. Rocks near reservoirs are already under a lot of pressure. The water adds even more pressure. This can set off faults nearby.

Mining can also cause earthquakes. Mining is when humans remove matter, such as gems, from within Earth. Miners have to dig tunnels to reach the matter they want. Digging deep tunnels near faults can be dangerous. It can add pressure to the faults. This can set off earthquakes.

THE HOOVER DAM CREATED A HUGE RESERVOIR IN NEVADA. IT HOLDS WATER FROM LAKE MEAD. SEVERAL EARTHQUAKES HAPPENED WHILE THE HOOVER DAM WAS BEING BUILT IN THE 1930s.

NUCLEAR EARTHQUAKES

Nuclear weapons can also generate earthquakes. These weapons give off huge amounts of energy. However, usually this energy isn't strong enough to affect Earth's tectonic plates. Humans have tested nuclear weapons underground. Seismologists study the seismic waves caused by nuclear weapons. This can help them tell if countries are testing nuclear weapons.

23

EFFECTS OF EARTHQUAKES

Earthquakes can make the ground shake and break. This is called ground shaking. It doesn't usually hurt people. But the effects certainly can. Ground shaking can break buildings and bridges. They can even fall down. If a building is sitting on top of a fault, it can be ripped in half!

Ground shaking can crack roads. It can leave streets broken up into pieces. These pieces can be at different heights. Ground shaking can also break gas lines. These are pipes of gas underground. It can also damage power lines, or cables that carry electricity. Broken gas and power lines can start fires.

ABOUT 250,000 PEOPLE LOST THEIR HOMES IN THE 1906 DISASTER. IT'S THOUGHT THAT OVER 3,000 PEOPLE DIED.

FIRE DISASTER

The San Francisco earthquake of 1906 was one of the worst in history. It had a magnitude of 7.9. It happened in the San Andreas Fault zone. The earthquake started a huge fire. It burned for four days. Finally, rain put it out. About 28,000 buildings were lost to the fire.

25

EARTHQUAKES CAUSE DISASTERS

Earthquakes cause damage through other natural disasters they set off too. Natural disasters are powerful events in nature that can cause a lot of wreckage.

Earthquakes that happen under the ocean can cause giant waves. These are called tsunamis (soo-NAH-mees). Tsunamis travel much farther onto land than regular waves. They can move as fast as a jet plane and can be more than 100 feet (30.5 m) tall. Tsunamis cause terrible floods.

Earthquakes can also cause landslides. This is when parts of hills or mountains on steep slopes fall off. They roll down the slopes. Landslides can knock over trees and buildings.

A 9.1-MAGNITUDE EARTHQUAKE CAUSED THE DEADLIEST TSUNAMI IN HISTORY. IT HIT SUMATRA, INDONESIA, IN 2004. THE WAVE WAS 60 TO 100 FEET (18.3 TO 30.5 M) TALL. IT MOVED ABOUT 5 MILES (8 KM) ONTO LAND.

WATER DISASTER

Earthquakes can mix dirt with water from under the ground. This is called liquefaction. It makes the ground very soft. Buildings can start to sink! Sometimes water mixes with landslides. This can make a powerful flow of mud. It can even cause a flood. Earthquakes can also cause floods by breaking dams.

27

EARTHQUAKE ENGINEERING

Humans can't stop earthquakes from happening. We have to learn how to live with them.

This has lead to some brilliant **engineering**. Some engineers look for ways to protect buildings and bridges from earthquakes. This is called seismic engineering.

Seismic engineers have found that buildings need to be flexible. This means they can move and bend. If buildings are too stiff, they can snap in an earthquake. Taller buildings are more flexible than short buildings. Believe it or not, a skyscraper is actually safer than a house in an earthquake!

Building on hard rock also helps. Rocks soak in seismic waves. This means fewer waves reach the building.

Earthquakes are always going to exist, but with smarter engineering, we can help lessen the harm they cause.

PHILIPPINE ARENA

THE PHILIPPINE **ARENA** IS THE LARGEST INDOOR ARENA IN THE WORLD. IT SITS ON A LAYER OF BASE ISOLATORS. THESE ISOLATORS ARE MADE TO MOVE DURING AN EARTHQUAKE SO THE BUILDING CAN STAY STABLE.

ALL ABOUT THE BASE

The base, or bottom, of a building is important too. Seismic engineers can put a **buffer** under the base. This protects the building from seismic waves coming up from Earth. It can also help the building move with the quakes. These buffers are called base isolators.

29

GLOSSARY

arena: a building with a large central area surrounded by seats, commonly used for sports and other entertainment

buffer: a layer of protection between two things

damage: harm. Also, to cause harm.

engineering: the use of science and math to build better objects

literally: in a completely true way

magma: a hot, liquid rock inside Earth

Mid-Atlantic Ridge: a mainly underwater mountain range in the Atlantic Ocean

molten: changed into a liquid form by heat

nuclear weapon: a weapon that releases a huge amount of nuclear energy

reservoir: a place where something is stored

vibration: a rapid movement back and forth

FOR MORE INFORMATION

BOOKS

Hoobler, Dorothy and Thomas Hoobler. *What Was the San Francisco Earthquake?* New York, NY: Grosset & Dunlap, 2016.

Owens, Meredith. *Earthquakes.* New York, NY: PowerKids Press, 2017.

Shea, Therese M. *Rocked By Earthquakes.* New York, NY: PowerKids Press, 2018.

WEBSITES

Earthquakes
www.ducksters.com/science/earthquakes.php
Learn more about earthquakes at this cool site.

Earthquake
www.kids.nationalgeographic.com/explore/science/earthquake/
Visit this fun site for more earthquake facts.

Living with Earthquakes
www.dkfindout.com/us/earth/earthquakes/living-with-earthquakes/
Get your seismic engineering on at this interactive site!

INDEX